FIREPLACES

CHIMENEAS

CHEMINÉES

KAMINE

authors
Fernando de Haro & Omar Fuentes

editorial design & production
AM Editores S.A. de C.V.

project managers
Carlos Herver Díaz
Ana Teresa Vázquez de la Mora
Laura Mijares Castellá

coordination
Emily Keime López
Verónica Velasco Joos
Dulce Ma. Rodríguez Flores

prepress coordination
José Luis de la Rosa Meléndez

copywriters
Gonzalo Ang - Flora Covarrubias Patiño

english translation
Angloamericano de Cuernavaca - Enrique Santiery

french translation
Angloamericano de Cuernavaca - Carmen Chalamanch - Marta Pou

german translation
Angloamericano de Cuernavaca - Sabine Klein

EDITORES   PUBLISHERS

100+ TIPS · IDEAS
fireplaces . chimeneas
cheminées . kamine

© 2012, Fernando de Haro & Omar Fuentes
AM Editores S.A. de C.V.
Paseo de Tamarindos 400 B, suite 102, Col. Bosques de las Lomas,
C.P. 05120, México, D.F., Tel. 52(55) 5258 0279
ame@ameditores.com / **www.ameditores.com**

ISBN: 978-607-437-220-5

Printed in China.

INTRODUCTION
INTRODUCCIÓN
INTRODUCTION
EINLEITUNG

The fireplace is a symbol of the comfortable and cozy home, and marks the area where one of the most pleasant places in the house can be found. Today, there is a wide range of home fireplaces, according to their design, the materials they are made of or the fuels they use, the most common being wood and gas. Something similar can be said about technological advances related to higher calorific yields and safety of operation. Because of this, household fireplaces can be integrated into current architecture, their designs being adapted to the characteristics of the house.

Interesting models of classic, modern and minimalist fireplaces are presented in this book. From this, readers can take the ideas that best suit their tastes and overall design projects. Of course, those who make and install them are professionals, essential to ensuring their smooth operation, since their construction and assembly must be done with care. With respect to fireplaces, in most cases architects are the best advisors; there are even specialists in the field. In general, fireplaces must be taken into account from the initial phase of house's construction.

Una chimenea es símbolo de una casa cómoda y acogedora, y hace de la zona donde se encuentra uno de los lugares más placenteros del hogar. Actualmente, existe una amplia gama de chimeneas caseras, en base a su diseño, a los materiales que las conforman o al uso de combustibles que emplean, siendo las más comunes las de leña y las de gas. Algo similar puede decirse de los adelantos tecnológicos, relacionados con mayores rendimientos caloríficos y con la seguridad de su funcionamiento. Por lo anterior, las chimeneas domésticas pueden integrarse en la arquitectura actual, adecuando su diseño a las características de la casa.

En este libro se presentan interesantes modelos de chimeneas clásicas, modernas y minimalistas. De aquí el lector puede tomar las ideas que mejor se adapten a su gusto y a su proyecto general de diseño. Dado que quienes las realizan y las instalan son profesionales, es esencial asegurar su buen funcionamiento, pues su construcción y montaje deben ser cuidadosamente realizados. En la mayoría de los casos, los arquitectos son los mejores asesores en materia de chimeneas, incluso existen especialistas para su realización. En general, las chimeneas deben tomarse en cuenta desde la fase inicial de la construcción de la casa.

Une cheminée est le symbole d'une maison confortable et accueillante, qui fait de l'espace où elle se trouve un des endroits les plus agréables de la maison. Aujourd'hui, il existe une grande variété de cheminées pour la maison, selon leur design, les matériaux et le combustible qu'elles utilisent, mais en général elles sont au bois ou au gaz. On pourrait en dire autant des progrès technologiques concernant leur rendement calorifique et la sécurité de leur fonctionnement. Ainsi, les cheminées des maisons peuvent s'intégrer à l'architecture actuelle avec un design approprié aux caractéristiques de la maison.

Ce livre présente des modèles intéressants de cheminées classiques, modernes et minimalistes. Le lecteur peut en tirer les idées les mieux adaptées à son goût et à son projet général de design. Étant donné que ceux qui les fabriquent et les installent sont des professionnels, il est indispensable d'assurer leur bon fonctionnement et donc soigner leur construction et installation. En général les architectes sont les meilleurs conseillers en matière de cheminées, certains d'entre eux sont même des spécialistes. Il est nécessaire de prendre en compte la cheminée dès la phase initiale de la construction de la maison.

Ein Kamin ist der Inbegriff eines behagliches und gemütliches Hauses und macht aus dem Bereich, in dem er zu finden ist, einen der angenehmsten des Hauses. Heutzutage gibt es eine grosse Auswahl an Kaminen, unterschiedlich im Design, im Material, aus denen sie gemacht sind, und in den Brennstoffen die sie nutzen, wobei Holz und Gas die üblichsten sind. Das gleiche kann man über den technischen Fortschritt sagen, was den geringeren Energieverbrauch und die Sicherheit betrifft. Daher können Kamine in die moderne Architektur integriert warden, wobei ihr Design an die Besonderheiten des Hauses angepasst warden kann.

In diesem Buch werden interessante Beipiele für klassische, moderne und minimalistische Kamine vorgestellt. Aus diesen kann der Leser die Ideen auswählen, die am besten seinem Geschmack und dem generellen Projekt des Hauses entsprechen. Es ist wichtig, ein gutes Funtionieren sicherzustellen, daher sollte der Bau und der Einbau sehr sorgfältig von Fachleuten vorgenommen werden. Meistens sind Architekten, wenn es um Kamine geht, die besten Berater, aber es gibt auch Fachleute, die auf Kamine spezialisiert sind. Generell sollten Kamine schon von Anfang an beim Bau eines Hauses eingeplant werden.

CLASSIC

CLÁSICAS

CLASSIQUES

KLASSISCH

A classic fireplace can go well with either period or modern decor. A room's fireplace gives warmth (the Spanish word hogar, meaning both "home" and "hearth", stems from this), as well as being a decorative element. Indeed, in winter the fireplace will warm the room, and in summer it can be decorated it so it dresses up and adorns the house. Technology, which is constantly evolving, offers more efficient and refined heating methods, but many people prefer classic fireplaces, with traditional designs and stone or fireproof ceramic brick materials, with the ability to withstand heat. To address this need, classic fireplaces are still an excellent choice, as they can produce a warm space with a rustic inspiration, even in a mixture of styles. A classic fireplace in a modern living room can be well combined with contemporary decor, if its shape, size or style harmonizes with the decorative line of the room.

On the following pages is a varied selection of classic fireplaces, framed by different interior designs and distinct architectural concepts.

Una chimenea clásica puede ir bien con una decoración de época, o bien, con una moderna. La chimenea en una sala brinda calidez, —de ahí surge el término "hogar"—, además de ser un elemento decorativo. En efecto, en invierno la chimenea servirá para calentar la sala, y en verano es posible decorarla para que luzca y adorne la casa. La tecnología, que está en constante evolución, ofrece métodos de calefacción más eficientes y refinados, pero muchas personas prefieren las chimeneas clásicas, con diseños tradicionales y materiales pétreos o tabiques refractarios, con capacidad de resistir el calor. Para atender esta necesidad, las chimeneas clásicas siguen siendo una excelente opción, pues pueden producir un cálido ambiente a un espacio con inspiración rústica, e incluso con una mezcla de estilos. Una chimenea clásica en un salón moderno puede combinar muy bien con la decoración contemporánea, si armoniza su forma, su tamaño o su estilo con la línea decorativa de la sala.

En las páginas siguientes aparece una variada selección de chimeneas clásicas, enmarcadas por diferentes proyectos de decoración y en distintas concepciones arquitectónicas.

Une cheminée classique va bien avec une décoration classique ou moderne. La cheminée dans un salon offre de la chaleur – de là le terme « foyer » – et elle est en même temps un élément décoratif. Ainsi, pendant l'hiver, la cheminée réchauffera le salon et pendant l'été on peut la décorer pour qu'elle fasse de l'effet et décore la maison. La technologie, qui est en constante évolution, offre des méthodes de chauffage plus efficiaces et raffinées, mais beaucoup préfèrent les cheminées classiques au design traditionnel avec des matériaux en pierre ou des briques réfractaires afin de résister la chaleur. Pour répondre à ce besoin, les cheminées classiques sont toujours une excellente option, car elles peuvent produire une ambiance accueillante d'inspiration rustique, ou même un mélange de styles. Une cheminée classique dans un salon moderne peut très bien combiner avec une décoration contemporaine, si on harmonise sa forme, sa taille et son style avec celui du salon.

Les pages suivantes offrent une sélection très variée de cheminées classiques encadrées dans différents projets de décoration et conceptions architectoniques.

Ein klassischer Kamin kann gut zu einer zeitgemässen, oder auch modernen Dekoration passen. Ein Kamin in einem Wohnzimmer spendet, von seinem dekorativen Aspekt abgesehen, Wärme. In der Tat dient der Kamin dazu, im Winter das Wohnzimmer zu heizen und im Sommer ist es möglich ihn su dekorieren, damit er zur Geltung kommt und das Haus verschönert. Die sich konstant weiterentwickelnde Technik bietet effizientere und feinere Heizmöglichkeiten an, aber viele Leute bevorzugen einen klassischen Kamin, in einem traditionellen Design, aus Stein oder Kaminziegeln gebaut, die der Hitze standhalten. Daher sind klassische Kamine immer noch eine gute Option, da sie eine warme Atmosphäre in einem rustikalen Ambiente, oder auch in einer Mischung verschiedener Stile, schaffen. Ein klassischer Kamin in einem modernen Wohnzimmer kann durchaus sehr gut mit der zeitgenössischen Dekoration einhergehen, wenn seine Form, seine Grösse und sein Stil mit der dekorativen Linie im Raum in Harmonie stehen. Auf den folgenden Seiten erscheint eine abwechslungsreiche Auswahl an klassischen Kaminen, inmitten verschiedenster Dekorationsprojekten und in unterschiedlichen architektonischen Konzepten.

TIPS - ASTUCES - TIPPS
- *The use of greenery helps to beautify the space.*
- *El uso de vegetación ayuda a embellecer el espacio.*
- *L'emploi de végétation aide à embellir l'espace.*
- *Pflanzen helfen den Bereich zu verschönern.*

The fireplace being at the level of the room's furniture visually integrates it with those who enjoy it.

La chimenea, a la altura de los muebles de la sala, la integra visualmente con quienes la disfrutan.

La cheminée, à la hauteur des meubles du salon, s'intègre visuellement à ceux qui en profitent.

Der Kamin, auf der gleichen Höhe wie die Möbel, wird optisch indie Sitzecke und mit deren Benutzern integriert.

Fireplaces often become the focal point of the room, especially when they are part of the main wall.

Las chimeneas se convierten a menudo en el punto focal de la sala, sobre todo cuando son parte del muro principal.

Souvent les cheminées deviennent le point focal du salon, surtout quand elles font partie du mur principal.

Kamine werden häufig zum Mittelpunkt des Wohnzimmers, besonders wenn sie Teil der Hauptwand sind.

TIPS - ASTUCES - TIPPS

- *Placing chairs around the fireplace creates a warmer atmosphere.*
- *Al colocar sillones alrededor de la chimenea se crea un ambiente más cálido.*
- *Les fauteuils autour de la cheminée créent une ambiance plus accueillante.*
- *Mit den Sesseln, die um den Kamin angeordnet sind, wird ein heimeliges Ambiente geschaffen.*

The combination
of light colors
on the walls and
furniture produces
the feeling of
spaciousness.

La combinación
de tonos claros
en muros y
muebles produce
la sensación de
amplitud.

La combinaison
de tons clairs pour
les murs et les
meubles produit
une sensation
d'amplitude.

Die Kombination von
hellen Tönen auf
Wänden und
Möbeln lässt den
Eindruck von Weite
entstehen.

TIPS · ASTUCES · TIPPS
• A room with a fireplace can be a catalyst in cold environments.
• Un espacio con chimenea puede ser un catalizador en ambientes fríos.
• Un espace avec une cheminée peut être propice dans un environnement froid.
• Ein Bereich mit einem Kamin kann ein kühles Ambiente mildern.

A fireplace can be placed in a different room, like the dining room or the library.

Una chimenea puede colocarse en un lugar distinto a la sala, como el comedor o la biblioteca.

On peut placer la cheminée non seulement dans le salon, mais aussi dans la salle à manger ou la bibliothèque.

Ein Kamin kann nicht nur im Wohnzimmer, sondern auch im Esszimmer oder der Bibliothek eingebaut werden.

TIPS - ASTUCES - TIPPS
- A fireplace's height can modify the proportions of a space.
- La altura de las chimeneas puede modificar la proporción del espacio.
- La hauteur de la cheminée peut modifier la proportion de l'espace.
- Die Höhe des Kamins kann die Proportionen des Raumes ändern.

TIPS - ASTUCES - TIPPS
- *A comfortable sofa bed and fireplace invite you to relax.*
- *Un cómodo sofá cama y una chimenea invitan a relajarse.*
- *Un canapé-lit et une cheminée invitent à la détente.*
- *Ein bequemes Bettsofa und ein Kamin laden zur Entspannung ein.*

In some cases, the fireplace flue may be tubular in shape, allowing the scenery to be enjoyed.

En algunos casos, el tiro de la chimenea puede ser en forma tubular y permite disfrutar del paisaje.

Dans certains cas, le conduit de la cheminée peut être en forme tubulaire, ce qui permet de profiter du paysage.

Der Schornstein des Kamins kann auch ein Rohr sein und damit erlauben, den Blick auf die Landschaft zu geniessen.

TIPS - ASTUCES - TIPPS

• *Whether lit or not, the fireplace can be part of the decor and complement other embellishments.*

• *Encendida o apagada, la chimenea puede ser parte de la decoración y complementarse con otros adornos.*

• *Allumée ou pas, la cheminée peut faire partie de la décoration et s'accompagner d'autres éléments décoratifs.*

• *An oder aus, der Kamin ist Teil der Dekoration, die durch andere Stücke vervollständigt wird.*

It is essential that a fireplace have a good flue so it can breathe properly.

Es esencial que las chimeneas tengan un buen tiro, es decir que respiren adecuadamente.

Le bon tirage des cheminées est essentiel, c'est -à-dire qu'elles doivent respirer de manière approprié.

Es ist wichtig, das Kamine gut ziehen, das heisst, das sie eine angemessene Luftzirkulationz haben.

TIPS - ASTUCES - TIPPS
- *A special place for storing firewood can be placed near the fireplace.*
- *Cerca de la chimenea puede colocarse un lugar especial para almacenar la leña.*
- *Près de la cheminée il peut y avoir un endroit spécial pour ranger le bois.*
- *In der Nähe des Kamins kann man einen speziellen Platz einrichten, um das Feuerholz zu lagern.*

The rectangular design converges in the hallway, fireplace and wood compartment, giving unity to the space.

El diseño rectangular converge en el pasillo, la chimenea y el compartimiento para leña dándole unidad al espacio.

Le design rectangulaire converge dans le corridor, la cheminée et le compartiment pour le bois, créant ainsi une unité pour l'espace.

Das rechteckige Design verbindet den Flur, den Kamin und den Platz für das Feuerholz miteinander und gibt dem Bereich ein einheitliches Aussehen.

Even in small
spaces there can
be a place for a
fireplace.

Aún en espacios
pequeños puede
haber un lugar
para una
chimenea.

Même dans les
petits espaces
il peut y avoir
de la place pour
une cheminée.

Selbst in kleinen
Räumen kann
man Platz für
einen Kamin
finden.

TIPS - ASTUCES - TIPPS
- *A fireplace can be integrated into a study or work space.*
- *La chimenea puede integrarse al lugar de estudio y trabajo.*
- *La cheminée peut s'intégrer à l'endroit pour l'étude et le travail.*
- *Ein Kamin kann auch in einen Arbeitsbereich integriert werden.*

In a country house atmosphere, a fireplace is a very common decorative element.

En una casa de ambiente campestre, las chimeneas son elementos muy comunes de la decoración.

Dans une maison d'ambiance champêtre, les cheminées sont des éléments de décoration très fréquents.

In einem Landhaus sind Kamine übliche Elemente in der Dekoration.

TIPS · ASTUCES · TIPPS
• A good grating at the base helps oxygen to enter and stoke the fire, besides catching the ashes.
• Una buena rejilla en la base ayuda a que entre el oxígeno y se avive el fuego, además de recibir la ceniza.
• Une bonne grille à la base de la cheminée permet l'entrée de l'oxygène qui avive le feu ; en outre, elle reçoit les cendres.
• Ein Rost auf dem Boden des Kamins versorgt ihn mit Sauerstoff, belebt das Feuer und lässt die Asche nach unten fallen.

MODERN

MODERNAS

MODERNES

MODERN

In modern-style homes, some interesting fireplace designs turn up which sometimes break traditional architectural standards, but which have definite decorative effects. Of course, in every case the fireplace is intended to be a hundred percent functional and to fulfill its basic purpose: to provide warmth to the area where it is located. Thus, the following pages include fireplaces without flues, openings or outlets, that project out into the space. There are others that are cauldron-style, that burn gas or ethanol, producing neither ash nor soot, that are two-sided, emitting heat for two areas of the house, or that are table-top fireplaces, among others.

However, what is noteworthy, and the main reason that these fireplaces are part of this section, is the modernist decor environment in which each appears, regardless of color schemes, materials and textures. They are all great creative ideas that can provide inspiration for those who want to have or modify a home fireplace.

En las casas de estilo moderno se presentan interesantes propuestas de chimeneas, que en ocasiones rompen los cánones arquitectónicos tradicionales, pero tienen un definitivo efecto decorativo. Desde luego, en todos los casos se busca que las chimeneas sean ciento por ciento funcionales y que cumplan su objetivo básico: dar calidez al área donde se ubican. Así, en las páginas que siguen figuran chimeneas sin tiro, abiertas o salidas —que se proyectan al espacio—; hay otras a modo de pebeteros; chimeneas de gas o etanol, que no producen cenizas ni hollín; chimeneas de doble vista, que emiten calor para dos zonas de la casa, y chimeneas de mesa, entre otras.

Sin embargo, lo que es digno de notar, y la principal razón de que estas chimeneas formen parte de la presente sección, es el entorno de decoración modernista en el que aparece cada una, independientemente de sus esquemas cromáticos, materiales y texturas. Son todas ellas excelentes ideas creativas, que pueden servir de inspiración para quienes estén deseosos de tener o de modificar una chimenea en casa.

Dans les maisons modernes on trouve des styles de cheminées intéressants qui rompent parfois avec les principes architectoniques traditionnels et possèdent un effet décoratif définitif. Évidemment, dans tous les cas, les cheminées doivent être fonctionnelles à cent pour cent et correspondre à leur objectif central : réchauffer l'espace où elles se trouvent. Ainsi, dans les pages suivantes il y a des cheminées sans conduite, ouvertes ou en dehors du mur – qui se projettent dans l'espace ; il y en a d'autres au style encensoir, à gaz ou éthanol, qui ne produisent ni cendres ni suie ; des cheminée à deux vues qui réchauffent deux espaces de la maison, et les cheminées de table, entre autres.

Toutefois, ce qui est digne d'intérêt, et la raison principale pour que les cheminées fassent partie de cette section, c'est l'environnement décoratif moderniste de chacune, indépendamment de ses schémas chromatiques, matériaux et textures. Elles sont toutes d'excellentes idées créatives qui peuvent servir d'inspiration à ceux qui ont envie d'en avoir une, ou de modifier la cheminée de la maison.

In Häusern in modernem Stil präsentieren sich interessante Vorschläge für Kamine, die manchmal mit den traditionellen architektonischen Vorstellungen brechen, aber zweifelsohne einen dekorativen Effekt haben. Selbstverständlich sollten Kamine in jedem Fall funktionell sein und ihre Hauptfunktion erfüllen: dem Bereich, in dem sie sich befinden, Wärme zu spenden. So werden auf den folgenden Seiten Kamine ohne Schornstein, Öffnungen oder Ausgänge vorgestellt, die in den Raum abstrahlen-; es gibt andere wie Schalen; Kamine mit Gas oder Ethanol betrieben, die weder Asche noch Russ produzieren; Kamine mit zwei offenen Seiten, die zwei Bereiche des Hauses erwärmen und, unter anderen mehr, Tischkamine.

Zweifelsohne ist erwähnenswert und der Hauptgrund warum diese Kamine im folgenden Teil erwähnt werden, die moderne Dekoration in denen sie zu finden sind, unabhängig von ihren Farbtönen, Materialien und Texturen. Alle sind hervorragende kreative Ideen für alle, die einen Kamin im Haus ein- oder umbauen möchten.

TIPS - ASTUCES - TIPPS
- In a gas fireplace, the flame can be regulated.
- En una chimenea de gas puede regularse la llama.
- Dans une cheminée à gaz on peut régler la flamme.
- In einem Gaskamin kann man das Feuer regulieren.

Gas fireplaces require no flue to remove smoke, which means greater flexibility in design.

Las chimeneas de gas no requieren tiro para expulsar el humo, lo que implica mayor flexibilidad en el diseño.

Les cheminées à gaz n'ont pas besoin de conduite pour expulser la fumée, ce qui donne une plus grande flexibilité au design.

Gaskamine benötigen keinen Schornstein für den Rauch, was eine grössere Flexibilität im Design erlaubt.

The wooden
walls with
recessed shelves
contrast with
the black
wall of the
fireplace.

Las paredes
de madera
con alacenas
empotradas,
contrastan con la
pared negra de
la chimenea.

Les murs en
bois avec des
armoires encas-
trées contrastent
avec le mur noir
de la cheminée.

Die Holzwände
mit eingebauten
Regalen bilden
einen Kontrast
zu der schwarzen
Wand des
Kamins.

TIPS - ASTUCES - TIPPS
• *A space can be complemented with colored objects, such as a rug or flowers.*
• *Puede complementarse un espacio con objetos de color, como una alfombra o flores.*
• *L'espace peut être complété avec des objets en couleur, comme un tapis ou des fleurs.*
• *Man kann den Bereich mit farbigen Objekten, wie einem Teppich oder Blumen, vervollkommnen.*

Because they use
neither chimneys
nor flues, gas
fireplaces require
less cleaning and
maintenance.

Al no utilizar
campana ni tiro,
las chimeneas
de gas requieren
menor limpieza
y mantenimiento.

Les cheminées
à gaz, qui
n'emploient ni
hotte ni conduite,
sont plus faciles
à nettoyer et à
entretenir.

Da sie keinen
Abzug oder
Schornstein
benötigen, sind
Gaskamine
einfacher zu
säubern und
instand zu halten.

TIPS - ASTUCES - TIPPS
- *The two-sided fireplace is useful, since it benefits two areas.*
- *La chimenea de dos vistas resulta de gran utilidad, pues beneficia a dos áreas.*
- *La cheminée à deux vues est très utile, car elle bénéficie deux espaces.*
- *Ein zu zwei Seiten offener Kamin ist sehr praktisch, da zwei Bereiche von ihm profitieren.*

This open, caludron-style fireplace is decorative, flexible as to its location and can be incorporated into an already-built home.

Esta chimenea abierta, como pebetero, es decorativa, da flexibilidad a su ubicación y puede incorporarse en un vivienda ya construida.

Cette cheminée ouverte, comme un encensoir, est décorative, son placement est flexible et peut s'incorporer à une maison déjà construite.

Dieser offene Kamin, wie ein Trog, ist dekorativ, kann beliebig umgestellt werden und kann leicht in ein schon fertiges Haus integriert werden.

TIPS - ASTUCES - TIPPS
- *The installation of a gas fireplace is faster and less expensive.*
- *La instalación de una chimenea de gas resulta más rápida y económica.*
- *L'installation d'une cheminée à gaz est plus rapide et économique.*
- *Der Einbau eines Gaskamines ist schneller und preiswerter.*

The size of a fireplace can be determined by the design, in addition to meeting the space's heating needs.

El tamaño de una chimenea puede quedar determinado por el diseño, además de responder a las condiciones térmicas del espacio.

La taille de la cheminée est définie par el design, et peut aussi répondre aux conditions thermiques de l'espace.

Die Grösse des Kamins kann vom Design abhängen, nur dass sie den Ansprüchen des Bereiches angemessen sein muss.

TIPS - ASTUCES - TIPPS
- *Burning fireplaces are a great decorative element.*
- *las chimeneas encendidas se vuelven un gran elemento decorativo.*
- *les cheminées allumées deviennent un grand élément décoratif.*
- *Ein brennendes Kaminfeuer wird zu einem attraktiven dekorativen Element.*

TIPS - ASTUCES - TIPPS

• A nice combination of dark elements contrasts with the light wall and window of this room.

• Una bonita combinación de elementos oscuros, contrastan con la pared clara y el ventanal de esta sala.

• Une belle combinaison d'éléments foncés contraste avec le mur clair et la grande fenêtre du salon.

• Eine schöne Kombination dunkler Elemente stehen in Kontrast zu der hellen Wand und dem Wandfenster in diesem Wohnzimmer.

The fireplace is part of the design of a contemporary living room.

La chimenea es parte del diseño de una sala de estar contemporánea.

La cheminée fait partie du design d'une salle de séjour contemporaine.

Der Kamin formt Teil des Designs in diesem zeitgenössischen Wohnzimmer.

Incorporating mini-fireplaces on independent bases can make a space attractive and give it warmth, despite its scale.

La incorporación de mini chimeneas en bases independientes puede hacer atractivo un espacio y darle calidez, a pesar de su escala.

L'incorporation de mini cheminées sur des bases indépendantes peut rendre attractif un espace, et lui donner de la chaleur, malgré leur petite taille.

Mini – Kamine, auf einer unabhängigen Basis, können einen Bereich attraktiv machen und ihm, trotz seiner geringen Grösse, Wärme spenden.

TIPS - ASTUCES - TIPPS
- Even in modernist designs, fireplaces can occupy an important place.
- Incluso en proyectos modernistas, las chimeneas pueden ocupar un lugar importante.
- Même dans les projets modernistes, les cheminées peuvent occuper une place importante.
- Sogar in modernen Projekten können Kamine einen wichtigen Platz einnehmen.

It can be a
good idea
to locate the
fireplace facing
the dining
room, so as
to enjoy some
warm table talk.

Puede ser una
buena idea ubicar
la chimenea
frente al comedor
para disfrutar
de una cálida
sobremesa.

La cheminée en
face de la salle
à manger peut
être une bonne
idée pour passer
un bon moment
à table après
le repas.

Es kann eine
gute Idee sein
einen Kamin im
Essbereich zu
haben, um eine
gemütliche Zeit
nach dem Essen
zu geniessen.

TIPS - ASTUCES - TIPPS
• Both the lamp and the fireplace illuminate and give warmth to the dining room.
• Tanto la lámpara como la chimenea iluminan y dan calor al comedor.
• La lampe et aussi la cheminée éclairent et réchauffent la salle à manger.
• Sowohl die Lampe als auch der Kamin spenden dem Esszimmer Licht und Wärme.

In this innova-
tive design, the
fireplace, resem-
bling a piece of
furniture, both
warms and sepa-
rates two areas
of the house.

En este novedoso
diseño, la chime-
nea que asemeja
a un mueble,
separa y a la vez
entibia dos zonas
de la casa.

Dans ce design
innovateur, la
cheminée,
semblable à un
meuble, sert
à diviser et en
même temps à
réchauffer deux
espaces de
la maison.

In diesem
unkonventionellen
Design trennt der
Kamin, der einem
Möbelstück gleicht,
zwei Bereiche des
Hauses, während er
sie gleichzeitig
erwärmt.

TIPS - ASTUCES - TIPPS
- *An exhibit case can be placed over the fireplace to display some objects.*
- *Pueden colocarse exhibidores sobre la chimenea para mostrar algunos objetos.*
- *Il est possible de placer des étagères au-dessus de la cheminée pour y exhiber quelques objets.*
- *Man kann über dem Kamin Raum schaffen um einige Objekte ausstellen.*

TIPS - ASTUCES - TIPPS
• A fireplace's dark background contrasts with the soft colors of the dining room.
• Una chimenea de fondo oscuro contrasta con los suaves colores del comedor.
• Une cheminée au fond obscur contraste avec les couleurs douces de la salle à manger.
• Ein Kamin mit dunklem Hintergrund steht im Kontrast zu den sanften Farben des Esszimmers.

In a place where people will spend longer periods, such as in the dining room, it is suggested that the fireplace be located some distance away from the occupants.

En un lugar de mayor permanencia, como el comedor, se sugiere que la chimenea se ubique a cierta distancia de los ocupantes.

Dans les espaces que les occupants utilisent pendant longtemps, comme la salle à manger, il vaut mieux que la cheminée soit placée à quelque distance des occupants.

In einem Bereich, in dem man sich länger aufhält, wie dem Esszimmer, sollte der Kamin in gewissem Abstand zu den Benutzern angebracht werden.

Regardless of the size of the room, a fireplace can look really good and, above all, give warmth to the area.

Sin importar el tamaño de la estancia, una chimenea puede lucir muy bien y, sobre todo, dar calor a la zona.

Peu importela grandeur de la salle de séjour, une cheminée peu faire de l'effet et surtout donner de la chaleur à l'espace.

Die Grösse des Raumes spielt keine Rolle, ein Kamin sieht gut aus und spendet dem Bereich Wärme.

TIPS - ASTUCES - TIPPS
- Gas systems allow fireplaces to be mounted on walls.
- Los sistemas de gas permiten sobreponer chimeneas en muros.
- Les systèmes à gaz permettent de placer les cheminées contre les murs.
- Die Benutzung von Gas erlaubt es, Kamine an einer Wand anzubringen.

TIPS - ASTUCES - TIPPS

• Conversation spaces can be created which benefit from the fireplace's warmth.

• Pueden crearse espacios para conversar, que se beneficien del calor de la chimenea.

• On peut créer des espaces pour bavarder et profiter de la chaleur de la cheminée.

• Es können Bereiche zum Plaudern geschaffen werden, die von der Wärme des Kamins profitieren.

Accompanied
by wall coverings
such as wood and
stone, this fireplace
becomes a highly
decorative element.

Acompañada de
recubrimientos
como madera
y piedra, esta
chimenea se
convierte en un
elemento alta-
mente decorativo.

Cette cheminée,
recouverte
de bois et de
pierre, devient
un élément très
décoratif.

Mit Holz und
Stein verkleidet,
wird dieser
Kamin zu einem
sehr dekorativen
Element.

The panel around the fireplace blends harmoniously with the rest of the wood elements.

El paño donde se encuentra la chimenea, combina armoniosamente con el resto de los elementos en madera.

Le pan de mur de la cheminée combine de manière harmonieuse avec le reste des éléments en bois.

Die Fläche auf der der Kamin angebracht ist, kombiniert harmonisch mit den übrigen Holzelementen.

TIPS - ASTUCES - TIPPS
- *The combination of textures and colors creates tranquility and sobriety in the room.*
- *La combinación de texturas y colores crea tranquilidad y sobriedad a la estancia.*
- *La combinaison de textures et de couleurs donne à la salle de séjour du calme et de la sobriété.*
- *Die Kombination von Texturen und Farben bringt Ruhe und Gelassenheit in dieses Wohnzimmer.*

In adjoining
spaces,
fireplaces and
other decorative
elements, in this
case plants,
allow the visual
definition of
different areas
of the house.

En espacios
articulados, las
chimeneas y
otros elementos
decorativos, en
este caso plantas,
permiten definir
visualmente
diferentes áreas
de la casa.

Dans les espaces
combinés, les
cheminées et
d'autres éléments
décoratifs, dans ce
cas les plantes,
permettent de
définir visuellement
les différents espaces
de la maison.

In verbundenen
Bereichen erlauben
Kamine und
andere dekorative
Elemente, in diesem
Fall Pflanzen, die
Bereiche optisch
zu definieren.

TIPS - ASTUCES - TIPPS
• With front and side openings, the fireplace's shape brings the spaces together.
• La forma de la chimenea con apertura frontal y lateral integra los espacios.
• La forme de la cheminée, avec une ouverture frontale et latérale, intègre les espaces.
• Die Form des Kamins mit seiner Öffnung nach vorn und den Seiten integriert die Bereiche miteinander.

Using the same material on the tables and wall coverings results in an excellent combination.

Al utilizar el mismo material en las mesas y en los recubrimientos de las paredes, se logra una excelente combinación.

L'emploi du même matériel pour les tables et les revêtements des murs achève une excellente combinaison.

Mit der Verwendung des gleichen Materials für die Tische und die Wandverkleidungen erreicht man eine hervorragende Kombination.

TIPS - ASTUCES - TIPPS
- *The walls can interplay with built-in or recessed elements for a nice composition.*
- *En los muros puede jugarse con elementos integrados o remetidos para lograr una adecuada composición.*
- *Sur les murs on peut jouer avec des éléments intégrés ou encastrés afin de réussir une composition parfaite.*
- *An den Wänden kann mit eingebauten oder eingelassenen Elementen gespielt werden, um eine angemessene Komposition zu erzielen.*

MINIMALIST
MINIMALISTAS
MINIMALISTES
MINIMALISTISCH

In the field of design, "minimalist" applies to that which has been reduced to the basics, to its essential elements. This word is derived from "minimum", and means "the least". Minimalist design has been influenced by Japanese simplicity. It is a movement or style that, speaking specifically of interior design, has gradually established itself in the West, until it has come to occupy a prominent place. The interest of minimalist designers is to give meaning to their designs starting with minimal elements, using lines, simple language and pure colors.

Therefore, presented in the following pages are some models of minimalist fireplaces, or those amidst minimalist environments, where the minimalist elements that have been preserved are enhanced, and naturally attract our attention.

En el ámbito del diseño, "minimalista" se aplica a aquello que ha sido reducido a lo básico, a sus elementos indispensables. Esta voz procede del inglés, minimalist, e implica lo mínimo. El diseño minimalista ha recibido la influencia japonesa de la sencillez. Se trata de un movimiento o estilo que, hablando concretamente de diseño de interiores, poco a poco se ha ido imponiendo en Occidente hasta llegar a ocupar un lugar destacado. El interés de los diseñadores minimalistas es dar sentido a sus diseños a partir de elementos mínimos, usando líneas, lenguaje simple y colores puros.

Por ello, se presentan en las siguientes páginas algunos modelos de chimeneas minimalistas, o en medio de ambientes minimalistas, donde quedan realzados los elementos que el minimalismo ha conservado y que de manera natural son los que atraen nuestra mirada.

Dans le domaine du design, le terme "minimaliste" est appliqué à tout ce qui a été réduit au minimum, c'est-à-dire, aux éléments indispensables. Il provient de l'anglais minimaliste et implique le minimum. Le dessein minimaliste a reçu l'influence japonaise de la simplicité. Il s'agit d'un mouvement ou style, qui, spécifiquement dans le design d'intérieurs, s'est imposé peu à peu en Occident, jusqu'à occuper un endroit important. Les designers minimalistes veulent donner un sens à leur design à partir d'éléments minimes, en utilisant des lignes, un langage simple et des couleurs pures.

Voilà pourquoi on représente dans les pages suivantes quelques modèles de cheminées minimalistes, ou dans des ambiances minimalistes, qui rehaussent les éléments que le minimalisme a conservés et qui, de manière naturelle, sont ceux qui attirent notre regard.

In der Welt des Designs, wird "minimalistisch" für all das verwendet, was auf die Hauptsache, auf seine unverzichtbaren Elemente, reduziert wurde. Das Wort stammt aus dem Englischen minimalist, und bedeutet Minimum. Minimalistisches Design ist von der japanischen Einfachheit beeinflusst. Es handelt sich um eine Bewegung oder einen Stil, der sich, konkret über das Innendesign sprechend, nach und nach in der westlichen Welt durchgesetzt hat, bis dahin, einen herausragenden Platz einzunehmen. Das Interesse der minimalistischen Designer ist es, ihren Entwürfen mit minimalen Elementen Sinn zu verleihen, in dem sie Linienführung, eine einfache Sprache und reine Farben verwenden.

Daher werden auf den folgenden Seiten einige Beispiele für minimalistische Kamine vorgestellt, oder welche in minimalistischen Umgebungen, in denen die Elemente, die der Minimalismus erhalten hat, herausstechen und die auf natürliche Weise unseren Blick auf sich lenken.

TIPS - ASTUCES - TIPPS
- *White-colored chairs, ceilings and walls help create a relaxed atmosphere.*
- *El color blanco en sillas, techos y paredes ayuda a crear un ambiente relajado.*
- *La couleur blanche des chaises, des plafonds et des murs contribue à créer une ambiance détendue.*
- *Die weisse Farbe der Stühle, Decken und Wände helfen ein entspanntes Ambiente zu schaffen.*

Installing the fireplace and appliances in a panel can save space.

Al empotrar la chimenea y los electrodomésticos en un panel, se puede ahorrar espacio.

Si on encastre la cheminée ou les électroménagers dans un panneau, on peut économiser de l'espace.

Mit dem Einbau des Kamins und der Haushaltsgeräte in einem Paneel, kann man Platz sparen.

In a minimalist and fuctional house, a fireplace has not only thermal but decorative objectives to meet.

En una casa minimalista y funcional, una chimenea tiene objetivos que cumplir, no solo térmicos, sino decorativos.

Dans une maison minimaliste et fonctionnelle, une cheminée a des objectifs à atteindre, non seulement thermiques, mais aussi décoratifs.

In einem minimalistischen und funktionalen Haus muss ein Kamin seine Aufgabe erfüllen, nicht nur die Beheizung, sondern auch in der Dekoration.

TIPS - ASTUCES - TIPPS
• There being few decorative elements, each detail takes on a significant importance.
• Al haber pocos elementos en la decoración, cada detalle cobra una importancia relevante.
• Quand il n'y a que quelques d'éléments dans la décoration, chaque détail a une grande importance.
• Da es nur wenige Elemente in der Dekoration gibt, ist jedes Detail von erheblicher Wichtigkeit.

White furniture
can complement
the living room
and the rest of its
elements.

Los muebles
en blanco pueden
hacer juego con
la sala y el resto
de sus elementos.

Les murs
blancs peuvent
harmoniser avec
le salon et ses
autres éléments.

Die weissen
Möbel passen
zum Wohnzimmer
und den übrigen
Elementen.

TIPS - ASTUCES - TIPPS
- Very different decorative styles can be used in the same space and still look like a harmonious whole.
- Pueden usarse en el mismo espacio estilos de decoración muy diferentes y aun así lucir como un todo armónico.
- On peut utiliser des styles de décoration très différents dans le même espace, et réussir malgré tout un ensemble harmonieux.
- Man kann im selben Bereich sehr verschiedene Dekorationsstile verwenden und selbst so zu einem harmonischen Gesamteindruck gelangen.

Thanks to its decorative elements, this smaller room can become a very cozy space.

Esta sala de reducidas dimensiones puede convertirse, por sus elementos decorativos, en un espacio muy acogedor.

Ce salon aux dimensions réduites peut, grâce à ses éléments décoratifs, devenir un espace très accueillant.

Dieses eher kleine Wohnzimmer wird durch seine dekorativen Elemente, in einen sehr gemütlichen Bereich verwandelt.

TIPS - ASTUCES - TIPPS
- The rocking chair by the fireplace gives a very endearing decorative touch.
- La mecedora junto a la chimenea da un toque de decoración muy entrañable.
- Le fauteuil à bascule près de la cheminée constitue une touche décorative attendrissante.
- Der Schaukelstuhl neben dem Kamin gibt der Dekoration eine liebenswerte Note.

Grey and steel tones give a cutting-edge touch to this white-walled living room.

Los tonos grises y acero, dan un toque de vanguardia a esta sala de paredes blancas.

Les tons gris et acier donnent une touche d'avant-garde à ce salon aux murs blancs.

Die Grautöne und der Stahl, geben diesem Wohnzimmer mit weissen Wänden eine avantgardisti-sche Note.

TIPS - ASTUCES - TIPPS
- *A wide fireplace can increase a room's proportions, while better distributing the heat.*
- *Una chimenea larga puede ampliar la proporción de una habitación, al mismo tiempo que distribuye mejor el calor.*
- *Une longue cheminée peut agrandir la proportion d'une pièce, et en même temps mieux distribuer la chaleur.*
- *Ein länglicher Kamin kann die Proportionen eines Raumes vergrössern und gleichzeitig besser die Wärme verteilen.*

The impression of a large fireplace is achieved, thanks to the dark band that serves as its background.

Se ha logrado dar la sensación de una gran chimenea gracias a la franja oscura que le sirve de fondo.

On a réussi l'impression d'une grande cheminée grâce à une frange foncée qui lui sert de fond.

Durch den dunklen Streifen im Hintergrund erscheint dieser Kamin grösser als er ist.

TIPS - ASTUCES - TIPPS
- *The wide fireplace and the two windows that look out into the garden amplify this space.*
- *La larga chimenea y las dos ventanas que dan al jardín amplifican este espacio.*
- *La longue cheminée et les deux fenêtres sur le jardin agrandissent cet espace.*
- *Der längliche Kamin und die zwei Fenster zum Garten vergrössern diesen Bereich.*

Through the arrangement of their furniture, some rooms are designed for admiring the fire in the fireplace.

Por la disposición de sus muebles, algunas salas están concebidas para admirar el fuego de la chimenea.

Par la disposition de leurs meubles, certains salons sont conçus pour admirer le feu de la cheminée.

Durch die Anordnung der Möbel scheinen manche Sitzecken dazu gemacht zu sein das Feuer des Kamins zu bewundern.

TIPS - ASTUCES - TIPPS
- *Placing some floor lamps, along with the fireplace and artificial lighting, can allow plays of light.*
- *Colocar lámparas de pie, junto con la chimenea y la iluminación artificial pueden permitir juegos de luz.*
- *Certaines lampes de pied, avec la cheminée et l'éclairage artificiel, peuvent permettre des jeux de lumière.*
- *Manche Stehlampen, neben dem Kamin und der künstlichen Beleuchtung, erlauben mit dem Licht zu spielen.*

A fireplace will always look great, regardless of the style of the house or furniture.

Una chimenea siempre podrá lucir, independiente- mente del estilo de la casa o del mobiliario.

Une cheminée fera toujours de l'effet, quelque soit le style de la maison ou son mobilier.

Ein Kamin kann immer gut aussehen, unabhängig des Stiles des Hauses oder der Möbel.

TIPS - ASTUCES - TIPPS
- The fireplace's location can help to heat several areas of the house.
- La ubicación de la chimenea puede ayudar a calentar varias zonas de la casa.
- L'emplacement de la cheminée peut aider à réchauffer plusieurs parties de la maison.
- Die Lage des Kamins kann dazu beitragen mehrere Bereiche des Hauses zu erwärmen.

A fireplace can be at once a focal point, a visual touch, a hallway, a divider and part of the decor itself.

La cheminée peut être en même temps point focal, couronnement visuel, vestibule, division et une partie de la décoration elle-même.

La chimenea puede ser al mismo tiempo un punto focal, remate visual, vestíbulo, división y parte de la decoración misma.

Ein Kamin kann gleichzeitig ein Blickpunkt, ein optischer Abschluss, Abtrennung und Teil der Dekoration, sein.

architecture arquitectónicos architectoniques architektonische

photography   fotográficos   photographiques   fotografische

adán cárabes - pgs. 52

alberto moreno - pg. 93

allen vallejo - pgs. 60-61

arturo chávez - pg. 69

© beta-plus publishing - pgs. 3, 6-7,

8 (bottom), 10, 16, 22-23, 25-27,

32-35, 38-39, 57, 70-71, 74-76,

80-81, 90-91, 94-95, 98, 102-105,

107-111, 113-120, 122-126, 128-131

gabriela ibarra - pgs. 30-31, 68

guadalupe castillo - pgs. 30-31, 68

héctor velasco facio - pgs. 4-5, 42,

72-73, 78-79

ilan rabchinskey - pgs. 36-37

jaime navarro - pgs. 54-55, 65

jorge silva - pgs. 20-21

lourdes legorreta - pg. 8 (top)

marcos garcía - pgs. 28-29

mark callanan - pgs. 49, 62-63

martín opladen - pgs. 40-41

mito covarrubias - pgs. 88-89

sófocles hernández - pgs. 66-67, 86-87

víctor benítez - pgs. 8 (center), 44-45,

82-83, 85

víctor tovar hernández - pgs. 58-89